# RODENT RASCALS

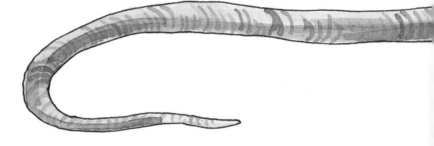

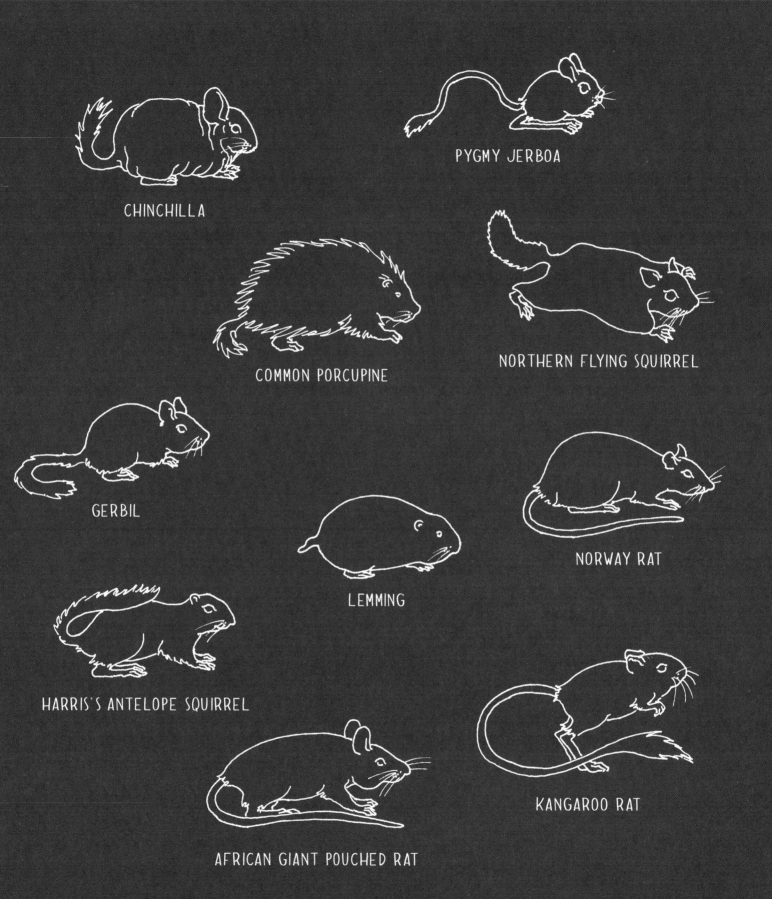

CHINCHILLA

PYGMY JERBOA

COMMON PORCUPINE

NORTHERN FLYING SQUIRREL

GERBIL

LEMMING

NORWAY RAT

HARRIS'S ANTELOPE SQUIRREL

AFRICAN GIANT POUCHED RAT

KANGAROO RAT

HAMSTER

MUSKRAT

NAKED MOLE RAT

CHIPMUNK

GUINEA PIG

HOUSE MOUSE

GREATER CAPYBARA

BLACK-TAILED PRAIRIE DOG

BEAVER

WOOD RAT

GROUNDHOG

# R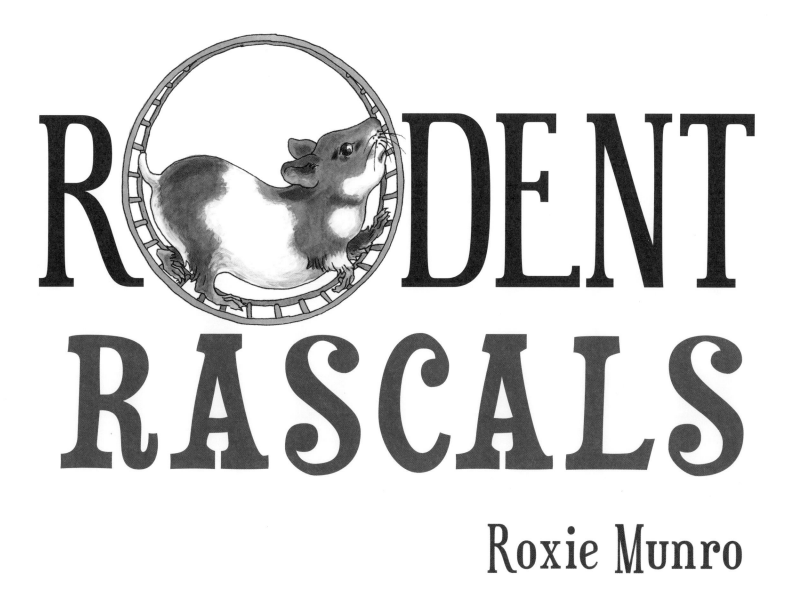DENT
# RASCALS

## Roxie Munro

HOLIDAY HOUSE  NEW YORK

*To Adeline Pearl Wood*

The publisher wishes to thank Neil Duncan, Collections Manager of the
American Museum of Natural History's Department of Mammalogy,
for his expert review of the text.

Library of Congress Cataloging-in-Publication Data

Names: Munro, Roxie, author.

Title: Rodent Rascals / Roxie Munro.

Description: First edition. | New York : Holiday House, [2018] | Audience:
  Ages 6-10. | Audience: Grades K-3. | Summary: "Life-size illustrations of rodent species
from around the world accompany simple, thorough text describing their life cycles,
sizes, habitats, and ranges"—Provided by publisher.

Identifiers: LCCN 2017019227 | ISBN 9780823438600 (hardcover)

Subjects: Rodents—Juvenile literature. | Rodents—Behavior—Juvenile literature.

Classification: LCC QL737.R6 M92 2018 |
  DDC 599.35—dc23

LC record available at https://lccn.loc.gov/2017019227

ISBN: 978-0-8234-4738-1 (paperback)

# INTRODUCTION

RODENTS really get around. Do you know about Hector, the astronaut rat? In 1961 France launched Hector 93 miles up into space. He returned safely to Earth. Hector wasn't the only rodent in space. Guinea pigs flew on an early Soviet Sputnik spacecraft. Eleven mice took off on a NASA flight in 1951. Now mice are living on the space station where they are part of experiments. Rodents, which also include squirrels, beavers, and porcupines, are much more helpful and brave than people realize.

What is a rodent? A rodent is a *mammal* with a single pair of teeth called incisors in both the upper and the lower jaw. These incisors never stop growing. Rodents keep them short by gnawing, a kind of self-sharpening. Rodents live on every continent except Antarctica. They have lots of different lifestyles. There are burrowers such as groundhogs and mole rats as well as tree-dwelling (or arboreol) and flying squirrels that take to the air. Some, such as capybaras and muskrats, are excellent swimmers, while jerboas and kangaroo rats are desert specialists. Solitary porcupines prefer their own company, but prairie dogs are highly social and live in large colonies.

Rodents come in many sizes. The creatures in this book are shown at their real size. These include the tiny African pygmy jerboa with a body that is smaller than 2 inches (about 5 centimeters) and that weighs only about as much as two pennies, as well as the huge greater capybara that grows to be more than 4 feet long (1.2 meters) and can weigh up to 200 pounds (90 kilograms). Enormous rodents known from fossils lived millions of years ago. The largest, *Josephoartigasia monesi*, had an estimated weight of 5,700 pounds (2,585 kilograms), which is as much as two cars!

Humans are lucky to have rodents. We use them as a source of fur, as pets, and in laboratory testing. Throughout history people have eaten them. Many still do. In ancient China newborn rats were prepared with honey as a delicacy. Today in some restaurants in China you can order black bean rat, rat soup with potatoes and onions, and a snake and rat dish. In Bordeaux, France, rats living in wine cellars drink wine, making them quite tasty when cooked in olive oil with shallots. Rat feet and tails are considered particularly yummy in areas of India. In parts of Mexico rats grilled or boiled into a stew are more popular than chicken. Other rodents can also become dinner. Roman emperors dined on baked dormouse stuffed with pork. In North America, squirrels and muskrats are still hunted and eaten. In South America, guinea pig is a welcome treat.

There isn't room in this book to include all rodents; they are the single largest order of mammals and include a wide variety of animals. Tunneling voles, which share many characteristics with muskrats and lemmings, are another type of rodent. There are also many more types of squirrels than the two in this book, including the red squirrel and the thirteen-lined ground squirrel. There are hundreds of mice species. One of the prettiest is the zebra mouse. Many people admire mice. The National Mouse Club of Britain awards prizes at mouse shows to the best examples of certain breeds, just as judges do at dog shows.

Rodents are a diverse group. Most are quite clever. These mammals have distinct characteristics, many different lifestyles, and one way or another are rodent rascals!

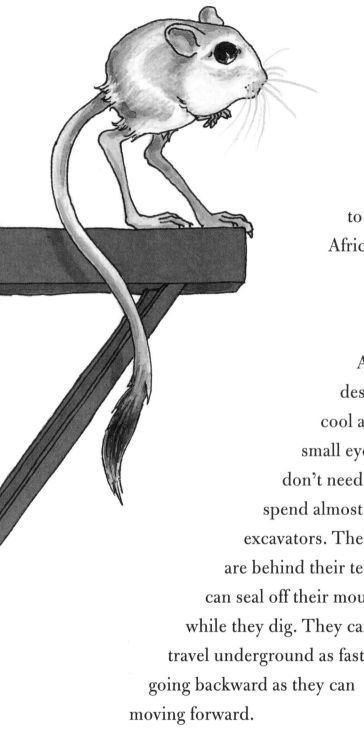

The tiny **pygmy jerboa** is the world's smallest rodent. They live in a desert *habitat*. It has such strong legs that it can jump up to 10 feet (3 meters), many times its length. They're as speedy as a fast human. Their quickness inspired Great Britain to name one of its World War II troop brigades in North Africa, where jerboas live, the Desert Rats.

Another odd creature living in the African deserts is the **naked mole rat**. To stay cool and safe, it burrows under the sand. Their small eyes give them poor sight, but these rodents don't need to see well in the dark tunnels where they spend almost all their time. Naked mole rats are expert excavators. Their lips, unlike ours, are behind their teeth, so they can seal off their mouths while they dig. They can travel underground as fast going backward as they can moving forward.

**Lemmings** burrow, too, but
under Arctic snow. These animals
don't really commit suicide by jumping
off cliffs into the sea as some say. It's an
overpopulation issue. When there are too
many lemmings in one place, a part of the group
must find a new territory. They sometimes drown
when large groups *migrate* across water.

**Hamsters**
make great
pets. They can
be trained to do
tricks, such as
jumping through
hoops and spinning
in circles. They love
to run and can go 5 or 6
miles on their wheel in a
day. They have bad eyesight
and are color-blind, but hamsters
can navigate by smell. They can also
feel by using their sensitive whiskers like
humans use hands.

The **house mouse** is a romantic. A male mouse
will sing squeaky love songs to his girlfriend. The
sounds are so high pitched humans can't hear
them, but apparently they're musical and like
birdsongs. A house mouse can hear sounds
we can't.

**Chipmunks** have huge pouches in their cheeks, like giant grocery bags. Their cheeks can expand to three times the size of the creature's head. Chipmunks work hard. They can collect as many as 165 acorns a day to store in their burrows for winter *hibernation*.

Small **Northern flying squirrels** can't really fly. They don't have wings. A thin fur-covered membrane that looks a bit like a wing stretches between their front and back legs. They can glide or soar as far as 300 feet (almost 90 meters). They steer with their legs and use their tails as rudders for direction while in the air and as brakes while landing. Giant flying Asian squirrels can be 2 feet (0.3 meters) wide, with an equally long tail. Some can travel as far as 1,500 feet (460 meters)—almost a third of a mile (close to half a kilometer).

There are about 110 species of gerbils, with names like vivacious gerbil, lesser short-tailed gerbil, pleasant gerbil, and the Indian hairy-footed gerbil. Most of these domesticated rodents descend from the Mongolian gerbil. These animals were brought to Paris in the nineteenth century and to America in the 1950s. They are gentle, social creatures and make great pets.

The cute little **desert kangaroo rat** can leap 9 feet (almost 3 meters), many times its length. It has big strong hind legs and large feet that are good for jumping in soft desert sand. It uses its tail for balance.

**Bushy-tailed wood rats** or pack rats love to collect bright shiny things, such as keys, bottle caps, and jewelry. If this big rat sees something more desirable than what it's carrying, it'll exchange one object for another. This habit has given it the nickname "trade" rat. Pack rats can be a nuisance—getting into attics, garages, and even car engines. They sometimes damage wiring and shred mattresses for their nests.

An amazing creature, the **Norway rat** is like a superhero. It can climb straight up a brick wall, jump off a 50-foot (15-meter) building and land on its feet, and walk on telephone wires, using its tail for balance. Its jaws are powerful, and its strong teeth can gnaw through practically anything: concrete several inches thick and even iron bars. These rats are smart

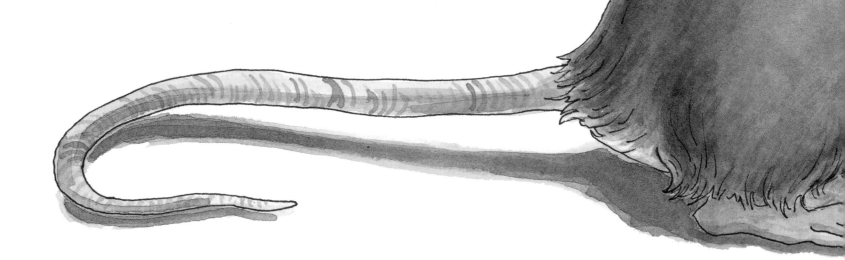

and have excellent memories. They have been trained to help electricians by dragging wires through walls. They are *omnivores*. One of the first owners of a pet rat was the children's book author Beatrix Potter, who wrote *Peter Rabbit*. Her pet was an albino bred from a single white rat caught in a graveyard by Queen Victoria's royal rat catcher, Jack Black.

**Harris's antelope squirrel** adapts well to the hot desert habitat where it lives. It holds its tail up to shade its back from the sun. This small squirrel engages in "heat dumping." It does this by lying down in a shady place on its tummy, flattening its body, and spreading its legs on the cool ground to release heat.

**Guinea pigs** are not pigs! A person used as a subject in research is often called a guinea pig. This is because for more than two hundred years actual guinea pigs have been used for biological experiments. These cute creatures are affectionate and very clean. Many have a "washcloth"—a little bald spot on the side of both front paws. They lick the spots to make them wet, and then groom themselves with their paws.

**Chinchillas** have soft fur so dense that water can't dry fast enough to prevent the growth of fungus. Instead of washing in water they take dust baths, rolling around in dust. The dust absorbs oil and dirt from their fur. Though they look chubby and not very athletic, they can jump up to 6 feet (almost 2 meters) high if a *predator* attacks. They have other defenses, too, like spraying smelly urine or releasing large clumps of fur, called a "fur slip," if they are bitten.

This vigilant guy is checking out the neighborhood from his observation post, a rim crater. It connects to a series of deep tunnels and burrows. This rodent is called a **prairie dog** because it barks like a dog to warn its large colony of family and friends of danger. Some scientists say a prairie dog's vocabulary is the most complex of any animal language. One type of prairie dog has different barks and squeaks for a coyote or a person or a bird coming into view. Prairie dog calls give specific information describing the visitor: what type of animal it is, how big, and how fast it's approaching.

Muskrats love water. Their back feet are partially webbed, and they have an unusual tail. The tail is slightly flattened vertically, which helps muskrats swim. Muskrats can swim backward or forward and can stay under water, including ice-covered areas, as long as 15 minutes. However, they're slow on land. They bring their food home and, like humans, eat on a dining room "table"—a flat elevated pile of mud and vegetation next to their living dens.

The most famous **groundhog** is Punxsutawney Phil. He lives in Pennsylvania and is known for predicting the weather. It's said that if, after waking up in early February from his winter hibernation, he sees his shadow, there'll be six more weeks of winter. If not, there'll be an early spring. Phil and his descendants have been forecasting the beginning of spring since 1886.

What's a "hero rat"? It's a trained **African giant pouched rat** that sniffs out dangerous, abandoned buried land mines. It has poor eyesight but an excellent sense of smell. Hero Rats are much less costly than dogs to train. They are safer to work with as well because their bodies are too light to detonate the explosives. Teaching the rats takes nine months, and at the end they have to pass a test with a 100 percent correct score to be able to work in the minefields. Their great sense of smell is even more helpful to humans in another way—giant pouched rats can detect tuberculosis. They can evaluate more lab samples with a higher accuracy rate in ten minutes than a human technician can in a whole day.

21

Baby porcupines are born with soft hairs, but within a day or two the soft hairs stiffen into quills. Quills are hairs coated with keratin, the same material that makes our fingernails. A single animal can have 30,000 quills. Porcupines don't send their quills into an enemy, as some people say. However, quills are easily released when they touch another animal. Embedded quills are painful to remove from, say, a dog's nose, because their tips have multiple backward-facing barbs, like tiny fishhooks.

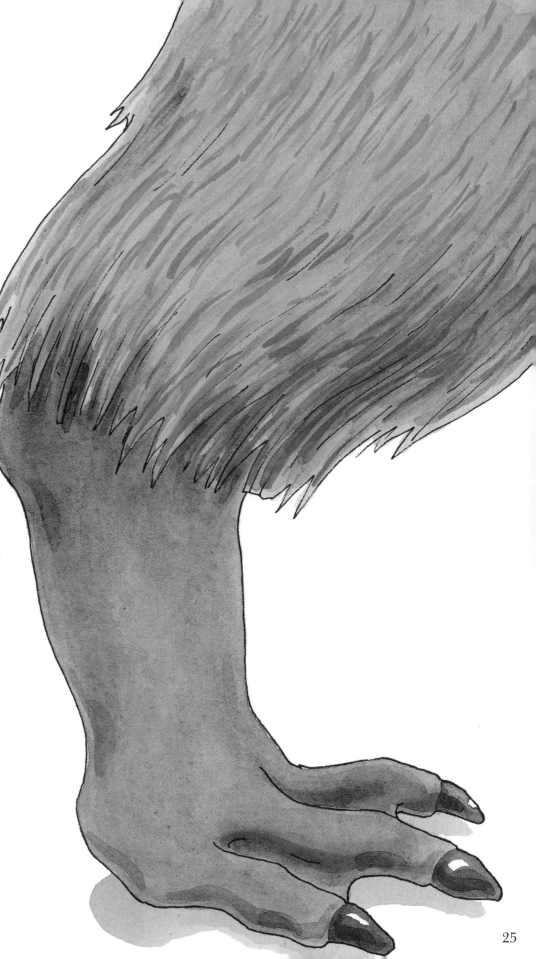

**Beavers** usually mate for life and are very family oriented. First they build a dam to make a beaver pond. Then the whole family works together to make a home out of branches and logs, stones, and mud. Part of a beaver house is above the water, but even the section underwater stays dry. The animals come and go from underwater tunnels dug in the floor. They're great swimmers, with webbed back feet. They can stay underwater for 15 minutes. Beavers have special flaps in their ears that close when they swim, two sets of eyelids that act like goggles, and even a mouth flap behind four big front teeth to keep water out when the beaver is carrying branches underwater.

This sweet-looking **capybara** is the largest rodent in the world. It lives in South America and is a gentle and friendly creature. It is a *herbivore*. It can be kept as a pet and has reportedly been trained as a seeing-eye guide animal for the blind. Capybaras are very social and live in large groups. They're quite vocal and can make sounds similar to a dog's bark, a horse's whinny, and a cat's purr. Capybaras love water, and as you can see, their eyes, ears, and nose are high up on their head, so they can stay almost totally submerged while swimming.

The **pygmy jerboa** (*Salpingotulus michaelis*) is the world's smallest rodent. Its body is 1.7 to 2 inches long (about 4 to 5 centimeters), with a tail 3 to 3.5 inches (about 8 to 9 centimeters). It's found in North Africa and Asia and is sometimes kept as a pet. Jerboas are *nocturnal*, *foraging* for food mainly at night.

The almost hairless body of a **naked mole rat** (*Heterocephalus glaber*) is 3 to 4 inches long (8 to 10 centimeters), with a 1.5-inch tail (about 4 centimeters). Native to the Horn of Africa, it resides in large family groups in elaborate underground tunnels, up to three miles long. The naked mole rat lives longer than any other rodent.

A true **lemming** (*Lemmini*) is 2.75 to 7 inches long (about 7 to 18 centimeters), with a very short tail. It lives in the world's cool northern areas: Scandinavia, Russia, and North America. Lemmings are active year-round, often staying under the snow in the winter.

A **hamster**'s (*Cricetinae*) body length can be from 4 to 7 inches with a tiny half-inch tail (10 to 18 centimeters with a tiny tail of 1.27 centimeters), though some *species* are longer than 13 inches (33 centimeters)! They're found in the wild in Europe, Asia, and the Middle East and are domesticated as pets. The golden or Syrian hamster is the most popular pet hamster.

The **house mouse** (*Mus musculus*) is found all over the world. Its body can be from 2.5 to about 4 inches long, with a 2.4- to 4-inch tail (or about 6 to 10 centimeters long with a 6- to 10-centimeter tail). With flexible joints and segmented bones, it can squeeze through a tiny space, like a crack under a door.

**Chipmunks** (*Tamias*), of which there are many different species, are found mainly in North America. Their body size ranges from 4 to 7 inches long (about 10 to 18 centimeters) with a 3- to 5-inch (around 8 to 12 centimeters) bushy tail. They're actually little squirrels, the smallest member of the *Sciuridae* family, and, like some of their relatives, hibernate in winter.

The **northern flying squirrel** (*Glaucomys sabrinus*) is almost entirely nocturnal, living in North American forests. Its length is about 8 to 11 inches (about 20 to 28 centimeters), including a flattened tail. Its ancestors go back more than 33 million years!

**Gerbils** (*Gerbillinae*) are usually between 6 and 12 inches (15 to 30 centimeters), including a tufted tail. They are native to Africa and Asia. There are many different types. Gerbils can have more than 20 different coat colors and are clean, gentle, very social, and hardy pets.

Desert **kangaroo rats** (*Dipodomys deserti*) are found in western North America. This creature lives alone in a burrow. It's nocturnal and has excellent hearing and very good eyesight. Adult kangaroo rats are about 14 inches long (33 to 35.5 centimeters), plus their tufted tail.

A **bushy-tailed wood rat** (*Neotoma cinerea*) is sometimes called a pack rat or a trade rat. It can be from 12 to 16 inches long (about 30 to 40 centimeters), plus a 5- to 9-inch (12 to 22 centimeters) tail. It's nocturnal and solitary, with one adult living in the nest. Pack rats are found in Mexico, the western United States, and parts of Canada.

The **Norway rat** (*Rattus norvegicus*) is also called a brown rat, common rat, street rat, sewer rat, Hanover rat, or wharf rat. Its body can be as long as 10 inches (about 25 centimeters), with a tail that is slightly shorter than its body. This rat is nocturnal, has poor eyesight, and is a good swimmer. It may have originated in China and now is the most common species of rat in the world, living on all continents.

**Harris's antelope squirrel** (*Ammospermophilus harrisii*) lives in desert areas of northern Mexico and the southwestern United States. Its body is 8.5 to 10 inches (about 22 to 25 centimeters) long with a 3- to 4-inch tail (about 8 to 10 centimeters). This squirrel is *diurnal*, lives in burrows that it digs underground, and doesn't hibernate.

Domesticated **guinea pigs** (*Cavia porcellus*) are also called cavies. The Incas, in South America, domesticated guinea pigs more than 3,000 years ago. They bred them as pets and for food and offered them as sacrifices to their gods. Cavies vary in length from 8 to 10 inches (about 20 to 50 centimeters) and don't have a tail. When they're excited, they jump straight up and down, called popcorning. Cavies whistle, whine, purr, rumble, chatter, squeal, and chirp.

**Chinchillas** (*Chinchilla lanigera*) first appeared more than 20 million years ago in mountainous areas of South America. They're popular pets, and domesticated chinchillas are also bred for their dense, soft fur, which is used to make luxurious coats. They are 8.5 to 9.5 inches (about 22 to 24 centimeters) with a 3- to 6-inch tail (about 8 to 15 centimeters). They're usually nocturnal and are quite agile, and they are great jumpers and climbers.

Black-tailed **prairie dogs** (*Cynomys ludovicianus*) are a type of ground squirrel. They're 12 to 16 inches tall (about 30 to 40 centimeters) and live in Mexico and the western United States in family groups called coteries. Their colonies or towns are made up of groups of coteries called wards. Towns are often dozens of miles long, are made up of complex tunnels, and have separate rooms for sleeping in the summer, a different room for the winter, a nursery for raising the young, a place to store food, and even a bathroom for waste.

**Muskrats** (*Ondatra zibethicus*) live in wetlands in family groups in lodges or dens along streams or lake banks. Muskrats are 16 to 25 inches long (40 to 62 centimeters). They were an important source of dense warm fur in the early twentieth century in America and were later introduced to northern Europe, Asia, and South America.

**Groundhogs** (*Marmota monax*) are also known as woodchucks or whistle pigs. They live throughout most of the United States and in Canada. They're 16 to 26 inches long (about 40 to 66 centimeters) and are solitary creatures that hibernate in cold weather. Groundhogs make complex burrows that have various chambers, including a bathroom.

**African giant pouched rats** (*Cricetomys gambianus*) have bodies from 10 to 17.5 inches long (24 to 45 centimeters) plus tails that are up to 10 inches (24 centimeters). It's called a pouch rat because, like a hamster or chipmunk, it can hold several pounds of nuts at a time in its cheeks to take back to its burrow. People who keep them as pets say they are intelligent, affectionate, and playful.

The New World, or common, **porcupine** (*Erethizon dorsatum*) is 2 to 3 feet long (about half a meter to a meter), with an 8- to 10-inch tail (20 to 25 centimeters)—the third largest New World rodent. Porcupines are good swimmers and tree climbers and can live a few dozen years. There are porcupines on every continent except Antarctica and Australia. The tiny barbed hook at a porcupine's quill's tip inspired humans to invent a new type of hypodermic needle that stays in place.

The **beaver** (*Castor*) is the largest rodent in North America. Its average weight is 45 pounds (20 kilograms), though some weigh more than 100 pounds (45 kilograms)! Their body is about 3 feet (about a meter) long, with a foot-long tail (0.3 of a meter). The largest beaver dam found (by satellite) is almost a half mile long and is twice as wide as Hoover Dam. Beavers have been around at least 12 million years.

The world's biggest rodent, the **greater capybara** (*Hydrochaerus hydrochaeris*), lives in South America. It can grow to almost 4.5 feet long (1.37 meters), two feet tall at the shoulder, and weigh up to 150 pounds (65 kilograms). Like the small guinea pig, a close relation also from South America, it doesn't have a tail. Capybaras live in groups of up to 50 or even 100 individuals. They can sit up like dogs but can't hold food in their front paws, unlike most other rodents.

## GLOSSARY

**Arboreal:** lives in a tree

**Diurnal:** active during the day

**Forage:** to hunt or search for food

**Habitat:** the natural home of an animal, such as forest, park, grassland, desert, or wetland

**Herbivore:** an animal that eats plants

**Hibernate:** when an animal remains inactive during cold months, often "sleeping" in a burrow or cave

**Mammal:** warm-blooded vertebrate animal with hair or fur; most give birth to live young and nourish them with the mother's milk

**Migrate:** to travel on a regular or seasonal journey to make a nest, find food, or mate

**Nocturnal:** active at night and asleep during the day

**Omnivore:** an animal that eats both plants and animals

**Predator:** animals that hunt other animals for food

**Species:** a particular type of animal or plant

## SOURCES

**Arizona Sonora Desert Museum**
https://www.desertmuseum.org

*Encyclopaedia Britannica*
https://www.britannica.com/search?query=rodents

*National Geographic*
http://www.nationalgeographic.com/search/?q=rodents

**American Museum of Natural History**
http://www.amnh.org/content/search?SearchText=rodents

**Partnership with University of Michigan**
School of Education, University of Michigan Museum of Zoology, and the Detroit Public Schools, supported by the National Science Foundation
http://www.biokids.umich.edu/critters/Rodentia/

Gibbons, Gail. *Beavers*. New York: Holiday House, 2013

Lunde, Darrin. *Dirty Rats?* Illustrated by Adam Gustavson. Boston: Charlesbridge, 2015

Marrin, Albert. *Oh, Rats!: The Story of Rats and People*. Illustrated by C. B. Mordan. New York: Dutton Children's Books, Penguin Young Readers Group, 2008

# WEBSITES YOU MIGHT ENJOY

## LEARN ABOUT RODENTS IN THE WILD

**The Critter Catalogue from the University of Michigan**
http://www.biokids.umich.edu/critters/Rodentia/Pet Rodents

**Wildlife Journal Junior from New Hampshire Public Television**
http://www.nhptv.org/wild/rodentia.asp

## LEARN ABOUT RODENTS IN THE ZOO

**Bronx Zoo**
https://bronxzoo.com/exhibits/mouse-house

**San Diego Zoo**
http://animals.sandiegozoo.org/animals

**St. Louis Zoo**
https://www.stlzoo.org/animals/abouttheanimals/mammals/rodents/

**World Association of Zoos and Aquariums**
http://www.waza.org/en/zoo/visit-the-zoo/rodents-and-hares

## LEARN ABOUT PET RODENTS

**American Veterinary Medical Foundation**
https://www.avma.org/public/PetCare/Pages/Selecting-a-Pet-Rodent.aspx

**Chinchilla Care**
http://chinchillacare.org/

**The Humane Society of America**
http://www.humanesociety.org/animals/
This website gives information about keeping gerbils, guinea pigs, hamster, mice, or rats as pets.

**Royal Society for the Prevention of Cruelty to Animals**
https://www.rspca.org.uk/adviceandwelfare/pets/rodents

**Troy Animal Hospital**
http://troyanimalhospital.com/2015/04/15/troy-vet-tricks-teach-hamster/Rodents in the Wild
This website gives advice on how to teach a hamster to do tricks.

# WEBSITES OF RODENT ENTHUSIASTS

**The American Fancy Rat and Mouse Association (AFRMA)**
http://www.afrma.org/

**The National Mouse Club of Britain**
http://www.thenationalmouseclub.co.uk/

**The Punxsutawney Groundhog Club**
http://www.groundhog.org/

# INDEX

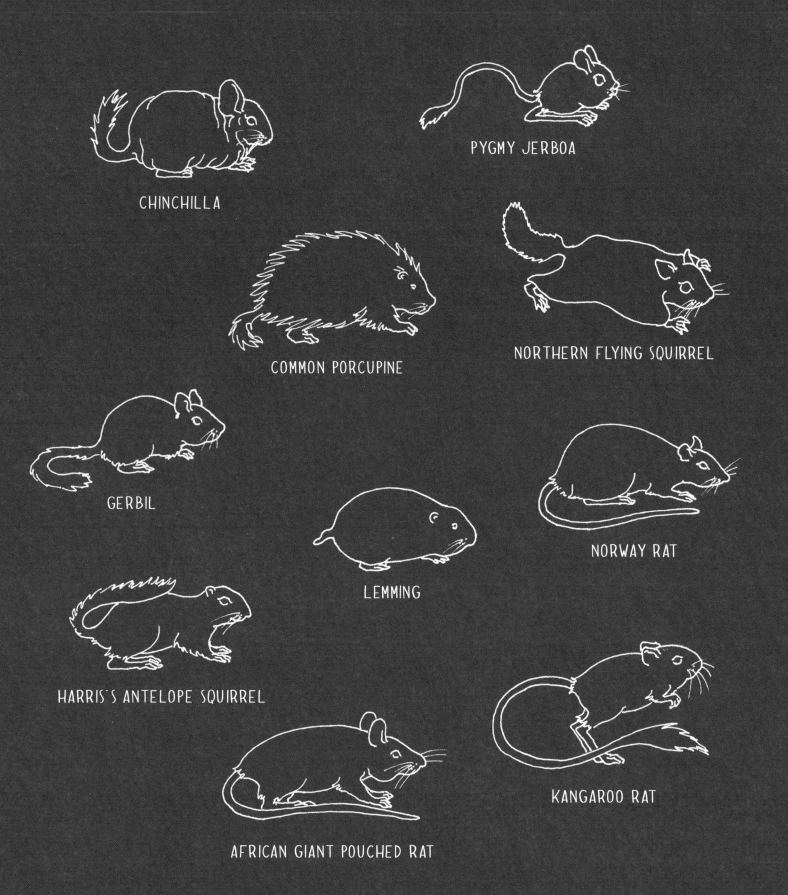

CHINCHILLA

PYGMY JERBOA

COMMON PORCUPINE

NORTHERN FLYING SQUIRREL

GERBIL

LEMMING

NORWAY RAT

HARRIS'S ANTELOPE SQUIRREL

AFRICAN GIANT POUCHED RAT

KANGAROO RAT

HAMSTER

MUSKRAT

NAKED MOLE RAT

CHIPMUNK

GUINEA PIG

HOUSE MOUSE

GREATER CAPYBARA

BLACK-TAILED PRAIRIE DOG

BEAVER

WOOD RAT

GROUNDHOG

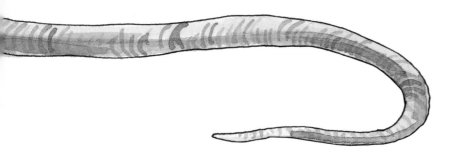